MW00625335

# THE 24 HOUR RULE

## LEADING IN A FRENETIC WORLD

CHARLES FRED

Susan Strecker, Editor
Todd Stansfield, Editor
Audra Gerber, Copy Editor

MAGNUSSON-SKOR®
PUBLISHING, LLC

Denver
www.mskor.com

Published by

Magnusson-Skor Publishing
Denver, CO 80237
***www.mskor.com***


Cover and book design by Fathom Creative Group.



---

Library of Congress Control Number: 2019930357

ISBN 9780999888827

First Edition

*My wife, Julie, among other things, is a talented potter. She takes a mitt full of hopeless clay and, with her bare hands and a few tools, creates a form both lasting and functional. She has been carefully guiding, shaping, and molding me for the past 40 years. May this book and its contents make her proud of her work.*

# Table of Contents

# THE 24 HOUR RULE

## LEADING IN A FRENETIC WORLD

# If You Only Have a Minute to Spare . . .

Is it possible that you would be a better person, a better leader, if you had full control over the variables impacting your life? Things like the economy, the weather, traffic . . .

Unfortunately, all remain beyond your ability to alter or change. But you do have complete control over one very important thing: how you respond and react to the stimulus from another human being. Regaining control of this element of your life will make you a better leader in our frenetic world. If you can believe this, then this book may be worth reading.

What I describe in this monograph does not require a major lifestyle alteration. Maybe a little more sleep, but for the most part, you can strengthen relationships and reduce the stress in your life and in your employees' lives by simply and deliberately finding a way to pause, a way to control how you respond to others. This emotional discipline is something we are all capable of but, sadly, few of us use.

We argue, with the help of some solid research, that stress, particularly stress that permeates an organization, is a mentally crippling force on people. The source of the stress often comes from when we act impulsively, without the emotional discipline necessary to control how we react and respond to a near-continuous provocation from a technical device. Our undisciplined responses and reactions come from an intractable mental model: *Get more done in less time.* It causes most of us to seek ways to compress more into our overfilled routines. Technology incessantly reminds us of this fact through interruptions, notifications, and alarms. There is no turning back, and the devices and apps we use today are bound to improve tomorrow. Unfortunately, when we search for examples of leaders succeeding amid the frenetic activity, we often discover the behaviors and lifestyles of famous billionaires. What we observe from these fortunate individuals is not replicable by mere mortals, yet many of us attempt to emulate them in vain.

It is important, before you read this book, that you fully understand my mission. Ambition, achievement, hustle, and exemplary performance are the true targets of this work. By encouraging pause as a discipline, I am not asking you to stop, delay, or even slow down, but rather to be intentional with your emotions and fully aware of your impact on others.

I truly hope you have a few more minutes—approximately 35, in fact. I purposely designed this work and message to fit into your busy day.

To get the most out of this book, I challenge you to take a few moments and reflect on the questions at the end of each section. The ⏸ is intended to initiate something you have complete control over.

# We Have Absolute Control Over One Thing

If you invest part of your life and read this book, I hope to provide three things.

First, I will describe something that is a personal treasure, and if I can translate it effectively, it may be valuable to you as well. Second, I'll expose an important leadership competency that has been muted by the frenetic pace of our world today. And third, I'll offer you a very simple discipline that could have a profound impact on your life and your ability to lead others.

To describe this thing I possess, let me ask you a question. Can you recall what you were doing on this exact day, one year ago? How about five years ago, ten, twenty? Since March 27, 1985—the day my first child was born—I have been contributing daily to a journal. In more than 34 years, I have only missed about 200 days. I'm now a full-fledged journal addict because I don't want to break the daily chain that has driven me to amass over 12,000 pages of entries. I've organized the journal with a taxonomy where I can identify the year, month, and day of my entries. There is a 98 percent chance I can tell you what I was thinking, experiencing, or learning on any given day over the past three decades. The discipline provides me the chance to look back and reflect on the full cycle of my decisions, what I was thinking at a different point in time, my assumptions and how they eventually played out. My early journaling captured awkward and nascent attempts to be a good husband and father of three.

For example, making the decision to coach my son's recreation-league basketball team. Teaching nine- and ten-year-old kids how to play basketball—as a team—is more difficult than it sounds. I came from a family where both my grandfather and my father were basketball coaches. One might imagine that I would have become a basketball player, given my gene pool. But I was only five feet tall as a freshman in high school. To my great surprise, my son was relatively tall for his age. So I thought I could redeem my life and pay homage to my ancestors by coaching my son toward basketball stardom.

We became the mighty Blue Panthers.

Since it was my first year as a coach, the kids assigned to our team were also first-year players. Suffice it to say, our talent was yet to be realized. We had 12 games that season, and unfortunately, we lost them all. However, in our last game of the season, we were tied, with a minute remaining on the game clock. We gained possession of the ball, and I called a time-out to prepare my little cagers for a play we had rehearsed in practice. In the huddle, I took the team through the diagram of our special play. I had a sense this was our big chance to finally win a game, to prove to the kids' parents that I knew what I was doing, and to give the boys a chance to experience the thrill of winning. I placed my hand in the middle of our huddle as we had done throughout the season. Each boy stacked his hand on mine. "Okay, on three," I shouted.

"Wait," said Joey, our point guard. He hadn't yet placed his hand in the center, and the other boys pulled back and looked at him. I first expected maybe he needed more clarity on the play or wanted to say something to inspire his teammates, but instead he asked, "Coach, what's the snack today?"

I've told this story countless times to get a laugh for his lack of focus at such a critical point. But my journal tells the rest of the story.

The team just wanted some assurance we had a pack of flavorful juice boxes and Oreo Double Stuf cookies like the week before. The boys, as I learned after the game, leaned on Joey to ensure the goodies would be available—critically important information, considering we only had a little time remaining in the game. But instead of simply answering his question, I stood from the huddle and shouted loudly enough for nearly everyone in the gym to hear.

"Get your head straight. All of you . . . we need to focus on the game!"

Joey looked at the floor; my son glared at me. The boys slowly walked toward our end of the court. We lost the game.

If I placed the pages of my journals side by side, they would extend 1.6 miles or the length of 28 football fields. The layout would theoretically display 34 years of note-taking in a single scene. Assuming I could walk along these pages and search for patterns, I would see change as a daily theme—the tumult, pain, and joy from life's churning cycle. Visible would be my efforts, in vain, to change or manage things completely out of my control. It has taken a lifetime to surrender to the many variables I can't regulate. And unfortunately, the one thing I have complete control over, I struggled to manage. I've learned that I can truly only regulate one thing: the way in which I respond and react to another human. The discovery is profoundly upsetting when I consider how many times I have avoided using the one power I have, especially when it injured another soul.

I would love to have a do-over with my

I'VE LEARNED THAT I CAN TRULY ONLY REGULATE ONE THING: THE WAY IN WHICH I RESPOND AND REACT TO ANOTHER HUMAN.

son and his teammates on that basketball court many years ago. Throughout the tattered journal pages are hundreds of human interactions I would like to have a chance to revisit. Unfortunately, the past is another thing out of my control.

As my children grew, so did my leadership responsibilities. Journaling allowed me to better understand my impact and influence on those I led and served. Five years ago, I initiated a research study to observe entrepreneurs of post-startup businesses (companies that survive and mature beyond the startup phase). My team of researchers wanted to understand why these businesses, which experienced early growth, eventually stagnated. Our study has now expanded to analyze over 4,000 businesses in the United States.[i]

This multi-year research effort identified a surprising yet perceptible pattern in the actions and behaviors of the leaders struggling with the growth and expansion of their businesses. We discovered a problem in the way employees approached their roles, solved problems, and interacted with each other; poor-performing firms showed working environments of

**POOR-PERFORMING FIRMS SHOWED WORKING ENVIRONMENTS OF INTENSE STRESS.**

intense stress. This problem was evident by the amount of unplanned turnover, employee disengagement, and chronically inconsistent financial performance. On a comparative basis, we were able to evaluate the influence of system-wide stress as we conducted hundreds of exit interviews with employees who had voluntarily left their employment. As a result of our study, the delta between high-performing firms and those struggling to grow was both qualitatively and quantitatively evident.

Our data pinpoints the source of this unnecessary stress. It falls squarely on the shoulders of those in roles that have influence over other people or over how teams and departments operate in the firm. Leaders single-handedly determine the stress levels of a business.

## LEADERS SINGLE-HANDEDLY DETERMINE THE STRESS LEVELS OF A BUSINESS.

I will highlight, in the next few pages, our findings of how stress is both mentally paralyzing and infectious, and if not abated, can destroy high-potential organizations.

***Do you believe you have control over your responses and reactions to others, specifically those you lead?***

Armed with my obsessive note-taking and our team's primary research, we set out to better understand how we can be more thoughtful and deliberate in how we respond to others. In concert with my team, I endeavor to reintroduce a competency for leadership that has been muted by the frenetic pace of our world and the endless reach of technology.

We present to you *The 24-Hour Rule* as a leadership discipline that inserts a pause into the reckless environment in which we live and work today. The discipline of *pause* focuses on the simple notion of creating a space between you and the persistent and perilous stimulus from a frenetic world. This safety zone sometimes only requires a few seconds—in other situations, a night of sleep. It can take a variety of forms, such as a deep breath, counting, a walk, meditation, sleep, or exercise. It doesn't matter what kind of pause we choose to adopt, only that it provides mental clarity and emotional discipline. Pausing resets our cognitive power, gives us more control, and provides crucial perspective. A conscious pause, especially by people in positions of authority, can fundamentally change a course of action, improve

Images, experiences, and beliefs greatly impact how we see the world around us. This is particularly true for aspiring leaders. The source of workplace stress is the tone, pace, and behaviors established by the leaders of an organization. But the cause is less about the personality of the leaders and more about how they perceive their role (their mental model) in a frenetic business climate.

Famed MIT professor Peter Senge made popular the understanding of mental models and how they influence behaviors and decisions. In general, a mental model represents how we perceive real or imaginary situations, and our perception is based upon past experiences and reinforcing actions. *Get more done in*

IN GENERAL, A MENTAL MODEL REPRESENTS HOW WE PERCEIVE REAL OR IMAGINARY SITUATIONS, AND OUR PERCEPTION IS BASED UPON PAST EXPERIENCES AND REINFORCING ACTIONS.

*less time* is an intractable mental model held by many business leaders. This belief is then reinforced by the stories of well-known billionaires running global businesses while competing in IRONMAN triathlons. These mythical beings don't need to sleep. We perceive that they have discovered a way to get so much more done in a day, and many of us want to be successful like them. So we shape our view of what is important and see that our role as leaders is to set a frantic pace for ourselves and our organizations.

Changing the mental model from fast to slow is not the aim of this book, nor would it eliminate stress. But a mindset of moving as fast as possible, getting more things done, and sleeping less is not working. When did we get into such a rapid pace that we have no time to reflect, learn, or deliberate? My journals are a solid source to find a point in time when the endless race began.

The May 2000 issue of *Fast Company* magazine had 414 pages and weighed almost three pounds.[iii] The Internet Economy, as we called it then, was in full bloom just before the big frost. The title of May's issue was "Speed Wins, How Fast Are You?"

IBM's "Speed Team" was the featured article, with pictures throughout the text of their executives running down hallways and lurching across a fictitious finish line. In hindsight, we know that technology was just beginning to radically change everything, and *Fast Company* was more right than wrong for the overtone of speed. However, since then, we've never decelerated enough to assess the overall impact of sprinting toward an indefinite finish line. We just keep running with the belief that faster must be better.

***Is your current pace sustainable?***

# The Discipline of Pause

The ceaseless evolution of technology combined with the unreachable outcomes of celebrated leaders underscores our need for a new mental model, one that enables us to *see* the role of a leader differently and confirms the value and impact of pause.

Pause is not a delay but a discipline. It's not a waste of time; rather, it affords us the time to deliberate before we act. It allows us to control how we respond and react to others, whether it takes five seconds or 24 hours. Most importantly, it does not delay our ambitions or dampen the need to hustle.

While we see relatively few exemplars of pause in today's world, they do exist. In fact, these examples live in the industries where every second carries the potential for life-threatening consequences and with professions defined by high stress. Take for example the commercial airline industry. Eighty-seven thousand flights take off and land every day in the United States.[iv] The industry has had a perfect safety record for 10 years; the last crash was in February 2009. Before a plane takes off in the United States, pilots and copilots pause and work collectively through a manual checklist, even though the computer has already done this for them. The practice started roughly 30 years ago, and while seemingly unnecessary, it works to perfection. Or consider the health-care industry with its practice of the surgical time-out. The Joint Commission[v] defines a time-out as "an immediate pause by the entire surgical team to confirm the correct patient, procedure, and site."[vi] Surgical teams have been using this protocol since 2003, greatly improving safety and health outcomes.

Both examples of pause save lives, and because of the potential consequences these high-risk industries face, they not only recognize the importance of pause, but they use and maintain systems that reinforce it as a standard of practice . . . as a discipline.

The role of a leader may not seem to carry the same immediate consequences as piloting an aircraft or performing surgery. Yet we directly influence the lives of the people we lead. I argue that the role of a leader is more diffi-

I ARGUE THAT THE ROLE OF A LEADER IS MORE DIFFICULT THAN THAT OF A PILOT OR SURGEON IN TERMS OF OUR POTENTIAL TO CAUSE WIDESPREAD HARM.

cult than that of a pilot or surgeon in terms of our potential to cause widespread harm. Unfortunately, leaders don't have a contained workspace or a controlled set of procedures to give us the method to pause. Instead, we begin each day with unknown situations, variables well beyond our ability to plan and prepare. For these reasons, a leader must use *self-discipline*—the ability to mentally call a time-out, to get rest, to run through a checklist—despite overwhelming temptations to quickly react or respond without doing so.

***How disciplined are you in scheduling time for pause? Could you schedule time on your calendar each day just for pause? A walk around your building? A great night of sleep?***

# Gaining Control

In his book *Essentialism: The Disciplined Pursuit of Less,* Greg McKeown argues that the people who accomplish the most every day don't send more emails or complete more tasks but instead focus on the few activities where they can make the greatest impact on their organizations and themselves. McKeown writes, "Essentialism is not about how to get more things done; it's about how to get the right things done. It is about making the wisest possible investment of your time and energy in order to operate at our highest point of contribution by doing only what is essential" (5).[vii]

Essentialism and pause share a common purpose. They both attempt to provide a direction toward mastering the things we can control. But where an essentialist has specific rules to declutter and eliminate tasks, the self-discipline of pause is different. We discovered early in our research that pause was not a simple topic for leadership training. Gaining control of how we respond and react to others involves deliberation and intention. Both behaviors are nuanced and require context and recognizing our assumptions. Each of us approaches this differently, so a prescriptive series of procedures is not a sustainable approach. Instead, we have found three fundamentals that can begin the process of developing the discipline of pause.

Start by being fully aware of stress in your work environment and how you may be contributing to the problem. Unlike a fish unaware

**GAINING CONTROL OF HOW WE RESPOND AND REACT TO OTHERS INVOLVES DELIBERATION AND INTENTION.**

it's in water, I believe stress is both measurable and obvious. Remember that the tone and pace of your organization is set by you. Next, make a commitment to pause, to gain control of how you react and respond to others. Let people know about it, discuss how difficult it is. The mere fact that you are openly self-aware with your team will reduce stress in the work environment. The last recommendation is to take a full week and try a few things that can help you gain control. This effort needs to match your personality and work habits. Write down what works and, more importantly, what doesn't work. Don't expect overnight changes in behavior, but do attempt this change with the same rigor as any other important goal in your life. After the week, take another picture of the stress in the workplace, and get your team involved in the conversation. Have them validate what things you've done to lessen the stress and anxiety in their work environment.

***Can you commit to pause? Can you lead this change in your team?***

# A Profound Impact

Her name was Maria. I met her during a week-long trip while attending a trade association conference. Maria was a housekeeper in the hotel where I stayed. I found the week unusually demanding. On the one hand, I held an active role at the conference, and on the other, I was trying to close financing for a company for which I was the executive chairman. The latter responsibility meant I needed to join a conference call every morning at 9:00 a.m., which I chose to take in my hotel room. It seemed more comfortable there; I could speak openly while avoiding the crowds of people attending the conference.

I got to know Maria because, oddly enough, at 9:00 a.m. every morning, she was somewhere in the hallway or in my room, cleaning. I noticed an uncommon quality in her. Despite working in a mundane, difficult job, she showed a great attitude. I could tell by the way she hummed, the way she went about her business that she cared about the quality of her work.

Then Thursday arrived. I found myself late for my call, and this time I was hosting it. I rushed from the conference center to the hotel, hoping to reach my room in time to initiate the call. As I approached the door of my room, out stepped Maria. Her eyes looked past me and quickly down at the floor. She didn't say hello or goodbye, just dashed by me quickly, grabbed her cart, and pushed it down the hallway. Stressed to get the call started, I didn't think much of my encounter with Maria.

I completed the call and entered the bathroom. My day was about to quickly change. I was six months into cancer treatment. As a part of my regimen, I took two forms of medication: a maintenance drug as part of ongoing therapy and another medication to control seizures I'd experienced as a result of the treatment. I took the former routinely and kept it in my pocket. I took the latter only when needed.

I kept the seizure medication in a small black travel kit, which I carefully placed next to the sink each time I left the hotel room. But now the kit sat on the edge of the counter, with the zipper open. I didn't want to approach the bag and look inside. I feared what I would discover, because this medication was a Schedule IV drug with considerable value to people without a prescription for its use.

I suspected the worst. And when I looked in the bag, I found it empty. Every sign and scenario told me Maria had stolen the drugs. I rushed to see if she and her cart were still in the hallway, hopeful I would find her and simply ask her to return the medication. But the hallway was empty, the time nearing 10:30 a.m.

I hadn't used this medication for more than a month, but the stress triggered some of the early signs of an oncoming seizure. I needed to catch Maria before she left the hotel. I hustled down the hotel hallway, thinking through the process of how I could find her. I entered the elevator and pressed the button for the lobby. At the last second, I stepped out before the doors closed. I realized the life-changing implications my actions would bring, greater than any seizure I could experience. Maria would be accused of a felony; no one would believe her over me. *What if Maria didn't steal the medication? What then?* Either way, it would ruin Maria's life.

I returned to my room to call my wife, Julie, a registered nurse and my care provider.

She listened as I tried to explain the situation. I could tell she detected panic in my voice, because soon I heard her rumble through the drawers in my bathroom, trying to find the medication.

"It's not there," I kept saying. "I remember packing it. I put the medication in my kit, like I always do."

"Wait a minute," she said. "You just got a new bag. Do you think it's in your old bag?"

"No. I cleaned out my old bag. It's in the garage."

"Let me try one more thing," she said.

I heard the door to our garage open and my wife unzip what could only be my old suitcase. Then she gasped.

"Oh my god," she said.

"You found them?" I shouted.

"I've got your pills right here."

Maria was in the hallway, on her typical schedule, the next day. She smiled warmly, said hello like usual, and continued humming while she worked. I have no idea why she didn't politely address me the day before, or why I left my travel kit open. What I do know is that I could have changed her life forever.

Pause. It carries a profound impact on people's lives. In today's high-paced environment, many things fall outside our control as leaders, which adds complexity to our positions. Markets change from day to day, the political climate shifts, and global warming continues to pose threats. Similarly, we cannot prevent a concert we're attending from getting rained out, traffic jams that offset meeting times, and employees suddenly quitting with no warning.

Yet through this turbulence of unpredictability and frustration, we retain complete command over what significantly contributes to the success of ourselves, our employees, and our organizations. We hold the power to decide how, when, and where we respond and react to crises, questions, criticisms, unforeseen situations, employees, and colleagues. When we exercise the discipline of pause, we inspire and lead others to accomplish remarkable feats that otherwise wouldn't occur. And when we don't, we allow external forces to influence our actions and potentially inflict untold and unknown harm on our people.

By taking a breath and mindfully making

WE HOLD THE POWER TO DECIDE HOW, WHEN, AND WHERE WE RESPOND AND REACT TO CRISES, QUESTIONS, CRITICISMS, UNFORESEEN SITUATIONS, EMPLOYEES, AND COLLEAGUES.

the decision to pause, we give ourselves, our businesses, and our people the best chance for success. My wish is that this book stays with you long after you turn the last page. May you finish our time together by closing this book and pausing before you get up to go about your busy day.

Thank you for spending this time with me.

# About the Author

Charles Fred is a bestselling author, serial entrepreneur, and 2019 Chair of the Association for Talent Development. He has devoted nearly four decades of his life to discovering new ways for professionals to acquire the skills necessary to compete in industries undergoing major transformation. Considered a pioneer in the e-learning industry, he has founded and led several successful companies that provide learning technologies and services. His bestselling book, *Breakaway*, is credited with introducing a new framework for organizational learning.

In 2000, Charles founded the Breakaway Group, one of the nation's fastest growing companies, to improve how health-care providers learn and adopt new technologies. Xerox acquired the Breakaway Group in 2011, and in the process, he became president of their health-care group, providing technology and services worldwide.

Today he focuses on the leadership role of second-stage entrepreneurs and their ability to create sustainable enterprises. TrueSpace, a firm he co-founded with his daughter Jamee, provides crucial know-how and capital for entrepreneurs aspiring to grow and reach the middle markets.

Charles is a longtime resident of Colorado, a journeyman cabinetmaker, and an elite masters track athlete. He and his wife, Julie, dedicate much of their time to their family, mentoring entrepreneurs, and giving back to the community.

## Magnusson-Skor Publishing

***Exclusively Publishing the Work of Entrepreneurs***

Magnusson-Skor Publishing is the exclusive partner of entrepreneurs seeking a platform to promote their thought leadership. We bring more than a decade of experience helping today's premier business leaders connect with audiences through best-selling books, keynote speeches, online media, and other outlets.

To learn more about MSKOR, visit:

***www.mskor.com***

[i] We have contracted with Gallup to assist in this multi-year effort.

[ii] Robinson, Joe. "Working Smarter: Why Stress is Contagious." *Optimal Performance Strategies*. https://www.worktolive.info/blog/bid/322776/why-stress-is-contagious.

[iii] The May 2000 issue of *Fast Company* magazine was the thirty-fourth monthly publication, with 414 pages. By comparison, the fifty-fourth issue, in January 2002, had only 89 pages.

[iv] "Air Traffic." *Science on a Sphere*. https://sos.noaa.gov/datasets/air-traffic/.

[v] The Joint Commission is a United States-based nonprofit tax-exempt 501 organization that accredits more than 21,000 US health-care organizations and programs.

[vi] The Joint Commission on Accreditation of Healthcare Organizations. *Comprehensive Accreditation Manual for Hospitals*. Glossary. Oakbrook Terrace, IL, 2017 update.

[vii] McKeown, Greg. *Essentialism: The Disciplined Pursuit of Less*. New York: Crown Business, 2014.

# Notes

IT DOESN'T MATTER
WHAT KIND OF PAUSE
WE CHOOSE TO ADOPT,
ONLY THAT IT PROVIDES
MENTAL CLARITY AND
EMOTIONAL DISCIPLINE.

and strengthen relationships, reduce stress, and save lives.

## PAUSE IS NOT A DELAY BUT A DISCIPLINE.

Pause is not a delay but a discipline. It's also not a one-size-fits-all solution but a practice that depends on the individual and the situation. My intention is not to offer a prescription to slow you down but to help you rediscover and embolden the power and control you have over the way you respond to and interact with other people.

***Is pausing difficult for you? What are some of your self-discipline strengths? Can you use them to create a moment of mental clarity?***

# The Stress Epidemic

Having emotional discipline and controlling how you respond and react to others takes a clear and deliberate mind. Few things constrain our thinking more than emotional pressure and stress. Stress, however, is not new, especially in a work environment. But periodic moments of stress and anxiety are different than the relentless burden to meet near-impossible expectations. Additionally, stress is contagious; it can be passed from one person to another just like a germ. We chose the term *epidemic* carefully because of the potential to overstate the problem. But when considering the sheer number of employees susceptible to multiple sources of the pathogen, we doubled down on our assertion. Like any outbreak of a germ or

virus, the way to stop it is to contain its source. To do so, we must first understand why we are not more emotionally resilient to stress, and why it is so easily spread from one person to another.

**LIKE ANY OUTBREAK OF A GERM OR VIRUS, THE WAY TO STOP IT IS TO CONTAIN ITS SOURCE.**

We are physiologically ill-equipped to deal with a modern version of unrelenting stress. Our bodies flush cortisol and adrenaline into our bloodstreams, giving us the heightened

ability to react quickly. These hormones direct blood flow to our muscles, especially our hearts. They prepare us in every sense to physically deal with the source of our stress in whatever manner gives us the best chance of survival. This stress response perfectly fit the world in which our ancestors lived, one where danger lurked everywhere and any encounter presented life-threatening consequences.

Yet as our world evolved, the rules of survival changed. Today, we live and work in an environment that demands less physical agility and more mental acuity. Rather than run faster or punch harder, we need to think more clearly and efficiently. And while yesterday's threats presented episodic life-threatening consequences,

today's stress comes from a nonstop set of pressures and emotions. This means our stress doesn't exist in the short time frame it takes to evade danger or fight a predator. Rather, it persists for days, weeks, months, or even years. Our stress also presents emotional consequences that can produce remorse, steal our sleep, and damage our health. While cortisol and adrenaline provided the apt fuel needed to survive in yesterday's world, these hormones stunt the very tool we need to prosper in today's environment: our cognition. So when we require mental acuity, we experience diminished recall. When we need sharp thinking and problem-solving, our minds are dull.

Researchers have long known stress is trans-

mittable; it's called the *stress contagion effect.*[ii] In addition to having hormones juicing our blood system, we possess mirror neurons that draw us toward the emotions of others. For example, when we hear others laugh, we smile. When we see someone yawn, we fight the impulse to mimic it. This urge is from brain cells with the specific purpose of copying the behavior of the person you are observing. As humans, we are perfectly designed to enable the epidemic of workplace stress. With hormones crippling our cognitive abilities, and neurons to ensnare those observing bad behavior, it is no wonder our research shows how quickly stress can become a workplace epidemic.

If the Centers for Disease Control and Pre-

vention (CDC) were to take the case of workplace stress, one of the first objectives of the investigative team would be to identify the source of the problem, and then eliminate it. When considering the source of an infectious disease, perhaps no other individual is more infamous than Mary Mallon, a teenage Irish immigrant who found work as a domestic servant upon arrival in the United States in the early twentieth century. She cooked for some of New York City's most elite families. She became known as Typhoid Mary after an outbreak of typhoid fever was traced to her cooking while she worked for a wealthy family vacationing in Long Island's Oyster Bay. Typhoid fever was considered a disease of the crowded slums, not of the

rich and famous. So Ms. Mallon, a poor servant living in a New York shantytown, became an easy target. She was, in fact, an asymptomatic carrier of the typhoid pathogen in that she had no symptoms of the illness. History reports that three people died as a result of eating her cooking and that 51 others were infected. She spent the last 26 years of her life in exile while hundreds of other asymptomatic carriers continued to walk the streets of the city.

To be infected by Mary, you needed to encounter her; in fact, you needed to eat the food she'd prepared and touched with her germ-ridden hands. The infectious nature of stress is different. Stress is airborne and technology-enabled. It lurks behind closed office doors

and hides within emails and texts, but it's omnipresent. Unlike its bacteria-laden brothers and sisters, stress can be sent at midnight across the globe from one carrier to an unsuspecting target with a perfect infection rate. The impacts of those affected are seen in unplanned turnover, lost time due to illness, and poor overall performance. Findings from our research study can isolate the carrier of stress in most organizations. The disease is spread from those who influence others in a leadership role; the most infectious are the leaders at the top of the organization. We can trace the virus from the exit interviews of employees leaving the firm, early-morning conference calls and late-night emails and texts. Like Typhoid Mary, most

leaders are unaware of their infectious behavior. They are, in other words, asymptomatic to the danger they pose to others. In interviews across the group of companies in our study, rarely did we deduct malice within the leaders regarding the spreading of stress and anxiety. In fact, most leaders believe they are setting a tone and an example for high performance.

## STRESS IS AIRBORNE AND TECHNOLOGY-ENABLED.

The asymptomatic nature of stress highlights a necessary but missing mechanism for leaders: a feedback loop. Leaders simply cannot see the destructive effect of their frenetic pace

and impulsive behaviors. Once stress begins to move from the leaders to the workforce, it spreads quickly. Consider the early signs of being infected. We have difficulty thinking clearly as the last email, text, or conversation occupies nearly every thought. Performance at a normal level becomes increasingly difficult and produces more stress, which only further diminishes our ability to perform. The often-used remedy for the infected is a job resignation, a way to leave the stress and its source behind. During our research period, we conducted hundreds of interviews from employees voluntarily leaving the companies we were studying. The exit discussions were a great ballast to the quantitative information we gathered concerning the per-

formance of the firm. I distinctly remember one of the interviews because it so clearly reinforced the pattern we were observing in organizations with widespread stress. I traveled to Chicago to meet with the employee; his name was Trevor. His exit was an unpleasant shock to the leaders of his company. We sat perpendicular to each other in the expansive main entrance of Chicago's Merchandise Mart. His company operated on the twenty-second floor of the Mart, and the public lobby offered a benign environment for our conversation. He was aware that I was working with his previous leaders, but I could tell he wanted to talk. He found a comfortable spot on an overstuffed chair and pecked at the nail on his ring finger.

"I want you to know," he stated, "the last five years have been great . . . but I just can't work like this anymore."

I said very little over the next 30 minutes; I didn't have to. He found an emotional outlet through our conversation and went on to describe a working environment of relentless stress and anxiety. He had been responsible for customer renewals, the annual re-contracting of clients using the mobile app developed by his company. The role was vital to the organization's future, and from what I deducted, he was a star at leading the team working with end users of the app and coordinating with the developers.

His story, from entry-level superstar to an

abrupt exit, unfortunately, was not a new one to our research team. The top leaders of his company were well-known entrepreneurs in Chicago. Working for them was considered a privilege and could build careers. Trevor, even to the day of his exit interview, was proud of the work he had done and those he worked for and with. He was not disgruntled, just emotionally exhausted.

Trevor's phone had become a self-inflicted torture device. He described texts and emails from his leaders in the middle of the night, and all days of the week. He began placing his phone next to his bed. Kudos were received the next day for waking and responding. Planned meetings would get disrupted by a text; the

subject didn't matter as much as who the text was from. He responded immediately if it was his boss, while those he was meeting with waited. Many days would begin with a 7:00 a.m. conference call because the CFO and the head of sales worked on the East Coast, and they'd end with a request from the CEO, who frequently traveled to San Francisco.

I asked Trevor why he didn't address his issues with those he worked for.

"I worked like this because I wanted to be just like them . . . and I thought I could be, you know . . . successful." The breaking point for Trevor finally arrived. As he described it, the environment put his mind into a vice. He couldn't think straight, lost his appetite, got

sick often, and found himself unable to keep up. A sense of not being able to meet the demand just increased his stress.

During the last part of our conversation, he shared how much relief he experienced after resigning. "I felt a huge weight lifted off my shoulders. For the first time in nearly a year, I slept through the night."

***Have you lost any people like Trevor due to the work environment? What can you, as a leader, begin to do to stop the spread of workplace stress?***

# The Need for a New Mental Model